Life Lessons Kids Should Learn Quickly

By

Brenda Diann Johnson

ASWIFTT ENTERPRISES, LLC
Duncanville, Texas 75138

Copyright © 2022 Brenda Diann Johnson
All Rights Reserved

No part of this book may be reproduced, stored in a retrieval system, or transmitted by any means, electronic, mechanical, photocopying, recording, or otherwise, without written permission from the author.

Brenda Diann Johnson
brendadiannjohnson@yahoo.com

Published by
ASWIFTT ENTERPRISES, LLC
Imprint: ASWIFTT BOOKS
P.O. Box 380669
Duncanville, Texas 75138

ISBN: 978-0-9910816-8-4

Library of Congress Control Number: 2022950572

Printed in the United States of America.

All scripture quotations are from The King James, American Standard, English Standard, New International, New Living Translation and The Amplified Version of The Bible. They are retrieved from biblehub.com and openbible.info/topics. All definitions are from Dictionary.com

Cover Design and Editing by Brenda Diann Johnson
Cover Photo © 2016 Syntika

Dedications

This book is dedicated to all children who deserve the best that God and our world has to offer in education and tools for the future. It is the responsibility of parents and guardians to provide basic needs such as food, shelter, clothing, safety & health. They must also provide the tools for physical and mental growth.

This book is also dedicated to parents, guardians, and mentors who are already taking responsibility to help guide our youth. It is our prayer that all children experience life's best and grow up to fulfill their God given DESTINY.

Acknowledgments

I want to acknowledge parents, guardians, schools, teachers, recreation center workers, caregivers, tutors, mentors, colleges, universities, trade schools, internships and other educational programs created to help students fulfill their goals and dreams. Our kids are assisted by many organizations that play a key role in helping our children make the best life choices.

Table of Contents

Dedications……………………………………………….....5
Acknowledgments……………………………………….6
Foreword……………………………………………………..9
Dear Parents………………………………………………..11
Introduction…………………………………………………15

Life Lesson 1: Learn The 10 Commandments………….....33
Life Lesson 2: Stay In A Child's Place……………….…....39
Life Lesson 3: Obey God, Parents & Authority…...……....47
Life Lesson 4: Show Appropriate Behavior………………..55
Life Lesson 5: Don't Mistreat Others………………………63
Life Lesson 6: Respect Others & Property…………….…..71
Life Lesson 7: Listen & Follow Directions………………..77
Life Lesson 8: Tell If Someone Hurts You………….….....85
Life Lesson 9: Seek Worthy Mentors……………………...93
Life Lesson 10: Don't Model Bad Habits…………….…....99

Conclusion…………………………………………………..107
Bibliography……………………………………………...111

About The Author…………………………………………..115
Books & Services…………………………………………...116

Foreword

I have known Brenda Johnson for fifteen years. From the first day I met her, I recognized a light, an abiding desire to help others grow, to blossom into the best versions of themselves. This was always particularly true for children — her students. Most importantly, they knew it, too.

For two years, we taught some of the same kids at a charter school. I made several visits to her media class with my students and observed her interaction with them. Her curriculum included topics that encouraged them to share their views as they broadened their horizons in journalism.

When I think of Brenda and what she brings to the table in the tumultuous state of our nation at this time, I am reminded of a quote from a most qualified personality in developing minds and hearts:

"Each of us, famous or infamous, is a role model for somebody, and if we aren't, we should behave as though we are—cheerful, kind, loving, courteous. Because you can be sure someone is watching and taking deliberate and diligent notes."

~Dr. Maya Angelou

Brenda is a cheerful, kind, loving, and courteous role model, guiding our youths with sound, appropriate keys to living a full, involved, honorable, and fulfilling life. She is a most viable role model, imparting life lessons to kids who are fortunate enough to have their paths cross hers. The late Dr. Angelou would be proud.

I personally feel blessed and honored to call such an exceptional woman my colleague and friend.

E. Rouchelle Washington
Educator and Author

Dear Parents,

This is REAL TALK and no DISRESPECT

Now that you have been delivered, set free from drugs, abuse, sexual addiction, murder, lying, cheating, stealing, gossiping, backbiting, racism, white or blue collar crimes, etc. and you have given your testimony how God saved you from the snare of Satan and has been good to you, "What About Our Children?"

You learned how to wage and fight the invisible warfare that the enemy planned against you and came out victorious. What are you going to do with your testimony of VICTORY? Again, I ask "What About Our Children?"

Our children are fighting an invisible fight everyday against an invisible enemy they are not equipped or experienced to fight. The enemy continues to come at them with tactics of drugs, abuse, illiteracy, high school dropouts, teen pregnancy, bullying, gangs, teen violence, guns, racism, promiscuity, AIDS, orphanhood, and children of divorced parents, sibling rivalry, broken parent and child relationships, fatherless and motherless children and more. But YOU know how to fight and win. YOU have proven it!

Join me in getting our children back to the basics by following and teaching God's principles for a victorious life. Become a mentor for kids, teens and young adults to help them navigate through the issues of life. Help them reach their God given DESTINY and become all that God has pre-ordained for their lives.

For His Kingdom,

Brenda Diann Johnson

Introduction

Introduction

A child's initial training ground to shape behavior starts at home. Parents are responsible for teaching their children manners, etiquette, social skills, rules and principles to interact with people and navigate through life successfully. Unfortunately, all kids don't get the same basic teachings because of various circumstances that exist in the home. No matter what misfortune kids face, respect of others, appropriate behavior, basic rules and principles are essential. Social skills, manners, etiquette, rules and principles are important for every child, teen and young adult. They should also be taught universal principles so they will know how to respond or act appropriately no matter what environment or setting they encounter.

During the kid stage is the time when kids learn new information. They are learning from scratch. Parents, guardians and mentors should give and model correct information and behavior to kids. The teenage stage is when teens are mentored and should follow the model of an adult who is responsible, has good moral character and integrity. At the young adult stage, individuals make independent decisions and apply what they have learned. In order to make good decisions young adults need a solid foundation which starts with the word of God found in the Bible. The Bible is the book of God's principles. Young adults will obtain wisdom and become more successful at making good decisions when they apply God's principles.

Parents, guardians and mentors should understand each stage of child development to adulthood. Knowing the stages of mental, emotional and physical development provides strategic tools that can be used when modeling important life lessons for kids.

According to the education philosopher, John Locke, babies are born void of information and their mind is a blank slate. The information given to kids is new training. Locke used the term "white paper" in his *Essay on Human Understanding*. The French translation uses the term "Tabula Rasa." It explains the human mind at birth is a blank slate and doesn't have processing information. Locke says rules and data are formed by sensory experiences that are later processed. (New World Encyclopedia)

Jean Piaget also describes the stages of early childhood development. He identifies the stage of cognitive and moral development in his writings. According to Piaget, humans can make sense of their environment through mental patterns that guide behavior and cognitive structures to process and organize information.

A child's cognitive development happens at different stages such as preoperational, sensorimotor, formal and concrete operational. From ages 0 to 2 children learn by imitation and memory which is the sensorimotor stage. At the preoperational stage children ages 2 to 7 develop the use of language and think operations through logically in one direction. From ages 7 to 11 children solve concrete hands-on problems in a logical way during the concrete operational stage. Children ages 11 to adult solve abstract problems in a logical fashion during the formal operational stage. Children become scientific in their thinking and have concerns about social issues and identity. (Mishra & Sing, 2019)

However, the education philosopher Erik Erikson wrote about children's self-esteem and how they socialize. Erikson said from infancy to adulthood a child's personality forms through 8 stages of psychosocial development. During each stage individuals have either positive or negative experiences that affect their personality.

Erikson also said it is important that individuals complete each stage to acquire basic virtues and develop a healthy personality. Basic virtues are character strengths that are used to resolve problems. When individuals fail to complete a stage, it affects other developmental stages that affect personality. Individuals can also complete stages later. (McLeod, 2018)

Basic virtues will not emerge naturally if something happens to interrupt the process of the psychosocial development from infancy to adult. The interruption has a negative affect in personality development. The individual will struggle in their sense of self until he or she recognizes their flaws and take responsibility to correct them. Many seek help by going to counselors or therapists to identify what happened in the past to cause their disfunction.

In Saul A. McLeod's research "Simply Psychology", he outlines Erik Erikson's eight stages of psychosocial development. He also shares what happens in each of the eight stages and the outcome. Each stage is divided by age from infant to adult. He identifies the virtues that emerge when each stage is completed successfully. McLeod also shares what happens when each stage encounters a negative experience.

According to Erikson there are 8 virtues that are supposed to emerge from infancy to adult. The first stage is trust versus mistrust which happens from birth to

18 months. The child depends on their mother or primary care giver for consistent care and stability. If the care the infant receives is predictable, reliable, and consistent, the child develops trust that he or she can carry to other relationships. The trust makes the child feel secure even in situations where he or she is threatened. Anxiety, fear, mistrust, and suspicion may develop if the child does not receive consistent care and stability. When the child successfully completes this stage, they develop the virtue of hope.

Autonomy versus shame and doubt is the second stage which happens from 18 months to 3 years old. The child is developing independence and personal control over physical skills. Parents should become their kids' biggest cheerleaders. They should encourage and support them. Adding value to your kids will help them become secure and confident in their abilities. When they feel secure, they can survive in the world. When parents do not add value and criticize, kids don't feel confident in their abilities to survive. They feel shame, doubt and have low self-esteem which makes them become dependent on others. Children who successfully complete this stage develop the virtue of will.

From 3 to 6 years old a child goes through the initiative versus guilt stage which is the third stage. The child becomes more assertive and asks more questions. Kids learn to make decisions and lead others when they feel secure and take initiatives. When kids are criticized, controlled and prevented from initiatives they feel guilty for being assertive. When the child successfully completes this stage, they develop the virtue of purpose.

The fourth stage is industry versus inferiority which happens from 5 to 12 years old. Children begin school. They start to read, write, and learn specific skills. At this stage children also seek approval from their peers. When children are praised and supported for taking action, they become confident, competent and industrious. They believe in themselves and achieve their goals. When children are not supported, they start feeling inferior to others. This has a negative affect on their potential to reach their goals. When the child successfully completes this stage, they develop the virtue of competence.

The fifth stage is identity versus role confusion which happens from 12 to 18 years old. During this stage is when teens transition from childhood to adulthood. They develop personal identity. Teens discover the roles they will play as adults.

They will also re-examine their identity. When teens don't discover their identity and their purpose in society it can lead to role confusion. When teens successfully complete this stage, they develop the virtue of fidelity.

From 18 to 40 an individual experiences intimacy versus isolation. During the sixth stage is when adults form intimate and loving bonds. When adults avoid intimacy because of fear of commitment it leads to depression, isolation, and loneliness. When adults successfully complete this stage, they develop the virtue of love.

The seventh stage is generativity versus stagnation which happens from 40 to 65 years old. During this stage is when adults start to give back to society. They want to leave their mark on the world. They also want to create or contribute to something that will outlast them. When adults feel successful for their accomplishments, they also feel useful. Failure makes them withdraw and they feel unproductive and stagnate. When adults successfully complete this stage, they develop the virtue of care.

Ego integrity versus despair occurs from 65 to death. This is the eighth and final stage. Adults often evaluate their past to see where they have failed or succeeded. When they didn't accomplish their goals or live out their dreams, they feel guilt and unproductive. They are disappointed and develop depression, hopelessness and despair. When adults successfully complete this stage, they develop the virtue of wisdom.

This book is 1 of 3 books. Ms. Johnson is also working on two more books titled "Life Lessons Teens Should Learn Quickly," and "Life Lessons Young Adults Should Learn Quickly." In this book she presents "Life Lessons Kids Should Learn Quickly."

Discussion Questions:

1. What does it mean to have hope?

2. A person of integrity means?

3. What are principles? Morals? Rules?

4. Why do people feel inferior to others?

5. What characteristics exist when a person has wisdom?

6. How can people display love to others? Give examples.

7. Why do people mistrust others? Give examples.

8. Why is the Bible important?

Further Study:

9 virtues in the Bible are discussed by Paul in Galatians 5:22-23, which are called the fruits of the Spirit which include love, joy, peace, patience, kindness, generosity, faithfulness, gentleness, and self-control. Explain each of these virtues and what they mean.

Definitions from dictionary.com:

1. Responsible----answerable or accountable, as for something within one's power, control, or management (often followed by *to* or *for*) 6. reliable or dependable, as in meeting debts, conducting business dealings, etc.

2. Integrity---adherence to moral and ethical principles; soundness of moral character; honesty.

3. Moral--- of, relating to, or concerned with the principles or rules of right conduct or the distinction between right and wrong; ethical.

4. Character---the aggregate of features and traits that form the individual nature of some person or thing. 3. moral or ethical quality.

5. Respect---esteem for or a sense of the worth or excellence of a person, a personal quality or ability, or something considered as a manifestation of a personal quality or ability.

6. Manners---a socially acceptable way of behaving.

7. Principles--a fundamental, primary, or general law or truth from which others are derived.

8. Rules---a principle or regulation governing conduct, action, procedure, arrangement, etc.

9. Social Skills---relating to, devoted to, or characterized by friendly companionship or relations. 4. living or disposed to live in companionship with others or in a community, rather than in isolation.

10. Etiquette---conventional requirements as to social behavior; proprieties of conduct as established in any class or community or for any occasion.

11. Wisdom--the quality or state of being <u>wise</u>; knowledge of what is true or right coupled with just judgment as to action; sagacity, discernment, or insight.

12. God---the Supreme Being, worshiped as the creator or ultimate source of the universe.

13. Bible---the collection of sacred writings of the Christian religion, comprising the Old and New Testaments.

14. Behavior---manner of behaving or acting. To act in a particular way; conduct or comport oneself or itself.

15. Personality---the visible aspect of one's character as it impresses others. 2. a person as an embodiment of a collection of qualities: 3. the sum total of the physical, mental, emotional, and social characteristics of an individual.

16. Self-Esteem---a realistic respect for or favorable impression of oneself; self-respect.

17. Trust---reliance on the integrity, strength, ability, surety, etc., of a person or thing; confidence.

18. Mistrust---lack of trust or confidence; distrust. 2. to regard with mistrust, suspicion, or doubt; distrust.

19. Autonomy---independence or freedom, as of the will or one's actions.

20. Shame---the painful feeling arising from the consciousness of something dishonorable, improper, ridiculous, etc., done by oneself or another:

21. Doubt---to be uncertain about; consider questionable or unlikely; hesitate to believe.

22. Initiative---an introductory act or step; leading action.

23. Guilt---the fact or state of having committed an offense, crime, violation, or wrong, especially against moral or penal law; culpability.

24. Industry---the aggregate of manufacturing or technically productive enterprises in a particular field, often named after its principal product:

25. Inferiority---the quality or state of being lesser or lower in rank, position, quality, etc. 2. the quality or state of feeling less important, valuable, or worthy.

26. Identity---the state or fact of remaining the same one or ones, as under varying aspects or conditions. 2. condition or character as to who a person or what a thing is; the qualities, beliefs, etc., that distinguish or identify a person or thing.

27. Role---the function assumed by a person or thing in a given action or process. 2. the rights, obligations, and expected behavior patterns associated with a particular social status.

28. Intimacy---a close, familiar, and usually affectionate or loving personal relationship with another person or group.

29. Isolation---to set or place apart; detach or separate so as to be alone. 7. a person, often shy or lacking in social skills, who avoids the company of others and has no friends within a group.

30. Generativity---capable of producing or creating.

31. Stagnation---the state or condition of stagnating, or having stopped, as by ceasing to run or flow. 3. a failure to develop, progress, or advance.

32. Ego Integrity---the "I" or self of any person; a person as thinking, feeling, and willing, and distinguishing itself from the selves of others and from objects of its thought.

33. Despair---loss of hope; hopelessness. 3. to lose, give up, or be without hope.

34. Virtues--- are character strengths that are used to resolve problems

35. Hope---the feeling that what is wanted can be had or that events will turn out for the best.

36. Will---desire, wish, decision, declaration, decree, choice, intent

37. Purpose----the reason for which something exists or is done, made, used, etc

38. Competence---having suitable or sufficient skill, knowledge, experience, etc., for some purpose; properly qualified.

39. Fidelity---strict observance of promises, duties, etc. 2. the state or quality of being loyal; faithfulness to commitments or obligations.

40. Love---a profoundly tender, passionate affection for another person. 2. a feeling of warm personal attachment or deep affection, as for a parent, child, or friend.

41. Care---a state of mind in which one is troubled; worry, anxiety, or concern

42. Wisdom---the quality or state of being wise; knowledge of what is true or right coupled with just judgment as to action; sagacity, discernment, or insight.

Scriptures on Hope:

1. For our light affliction, which is but for a moment, is working for us a far more exceeding and eternal weight of glory, while we do not look at the things which are seen, but at the things which are not seen. For the things which are seen are temporary, but the things which are not seen are eternal. (2 Corinthians 4:17-18)

2. Beloved, now we are children of God; and it has not yet been revealed what we shall be, but we know that when He is revealed, we shall be like Him, for we shall see Him as He is. And everyone who has this hope in Him purifies himself, just as He is pure. (1 John 3:2-3)

3. For I know the thoughts that I think toward you, says the Lord, thoughts of peace and not of evil, to give you a future and a hope. (Jeremiah 29:11)

4. Blessed is the man who trusts in the Lord, and whose hope is the Lord. For he shall be like a tree planted by the waters, which spreads out its roots by the river, and will not fear when heat comes: but its leaf will be green, and will not be anxious in the year of drought, nor will cease from yielding fruit. (Jeremiah 17:7-8)

5. Now hope does not disappoint, because the love of God has been poured out in our hearts by the Holy Spirit who was given to us. (Romans 5:5)

6. Now faith is the substance of things hoped for, the evidence of things not seen. (Hebrews 11:1)

Scriptures on Will/Desire:

1. The heart of man plans his way, but the Lord establishes his steps. (Proverbs 16:9)

2. And if it is evil in your eyes to serve the Lord, choose this day whom you will serve, whether the gods your fathers served in the region beyond the River, or the gods of the Amorites in whose land you dwell. But as for me and my house, we will serve the Lord. (Joshua 24:15)

3. If anyone's will is to do God's will, he will know whether the teaching is from God or whether I am speaking on my own authority. (John 7:17)

4. Behold, I stand at the door and knock. If anyone hears my voice and opens the door, I will come into him and eat with him, and he with me. (Revelation 3:20)

5. No temptation has overtaken you that is not common to man. God is faithful, and he will not let you be tempted beyond your ability, but with the temptation he will also provide the way of escape, that you may be able to endure it. (1 Corinthians 10:13)

6. The natural person does not accept the things of the Spirit of God, for they are folly to him, and he is not able to understand them because they are spiritually discerned. (1 Corinthians 2:14)

7. Who desires all people to be saved and to come to the knowledge of the truth. (1 Timothy 2:4)

8. The Lord is not slow to fulfill his promise as some count slowness, but is patient toward you, not wishing that any should perish, but that all should reach repentance. (2 Peter 3:9)

9. But we ought always to give thanks to God for you, brothers beloved by the Lord, because God chose you as the first fruits to be saved, through sanctification by the Spirit and belief in the truth. (2 Thessalonians 2:13)

10. Who saved us and called us to a holy calling, not because of our works but because of his own purpose and grace, which he gave us in Christ Jesus before the ages began. (2 Timothy 1:9)

11. And they may come to their senses and escape from the snare of the devil, after being captured by him to do his will. (2 Timothy 2:26)

12. I call heaven and earth to witness against you today, that I have set before you life and death, blessing and curse. Therefore, choose life, that you and your offspring may live. (Deuteronomy 30:19)

Scriptures on Purpose:

1. Many are the plans in a person's heart, but it is the Lord's purpose that prevails. (Proverbs 19:21)

2. A person's steps are directed by the Lord. How then can anyone understand their own way? (Proverbs 20:24 NIV)

3. For in Him all things were created: things in heaven and on earth, visible and invisible, whether thrones or powers or rulers or authorities; all things have been created through Him and for Him. (Colossians 1:16)

4. And He who searches our hearts knows the mind of the Spirit, because the Spirit intercedes for God's people in accordance with the will of God. (Romans 8:27 NIV)

5. There is a time for everything, and a season for every activity under the heavens. (Ecclesiastes 3:1)
6. My times are in Your hands; deliver me from the hands of my enemies, from those who pursue me. (Psalm 31:15 NIV)

7. Now to Him who is able to do immeasurably more than all we ask or imagine, according to His power that is at work within us. (Ephesians 3:20 NIV)

8. I know that You can do all things; no purpose of Yours can be thwarted. (Job 42:2)

9. Then you will understand what is right and just and fair - every good path. (Proverbs 2:9 NIV)

10. For those God foreknew He also predestined to be conformed to the image of His Son, that he might be the firstborn among many brothers and sisters. And those He predestined, He also calls; those He called, He also justified; those He justified, He also glorified. (Romans 8:29 NIV)

11. I make known the end from the beginning and from ancient times, what is still to come,' I say, 'My purpose will stand, and I will do all that I please. From the east I summon a bird of prey; from a far-off land, a man to fulfill my purpose. What I have said that I will bring about; what I have planned, that I will do. (Isaiah 46:10-11 NIV)

12. But the plans of the Lord stand firm forever, the purposes of His heart through all generations. (Psalm 33:11)

Bible Scriptures on Competence:

1. That the man of God may be competent, equipped for every good work. (2 Timothy 3:17 ESV)

2. Do your best to present yourself to God as one approved, a worker who has no need to be ashamed, rightly handling the word of truth. (2 Timothy 2:15 ESV)

3. Such is the confidence that we have through Christ toward God. Not that we are sufficient in ourselves to claim anything as coming from us, but our sufficiency is from God, (2 Corinthians 3:4-5 ESV)

4. My son, do not lose sight of these keep sound wisdom and discretion, (Proverbs 3:21 ESV)

5. Train up a child in the way he should go; even when he is old, he will not depart from it. (Proverbs 22:6 ESV)

6. Blessed is the man who walks not in the counsel of the wicked, nor stands in the way of sinners, nor sits in the seat of scoffers; but his delight is in the law of the LORD, and on his law, he meditates day and night. He is like a tree planted by streams of water that yields its fruit in its season, and its leaf does not wither. In all that he does, he prospers. The wicked are not so but are

like chaff that the wind drives away. Therefore the wicked will not stand in the judgment, nor sinners in the congregation of the righteous; ... (Psalm 1:1-36:1 ESV)

7. Trust in the LORD with all your heart, and do not lean on your own understanding. In all your ways acknowledge him, and he will make straight your paths. (Proverbs 3:5-6 ESV)

8. Do you see a man skillful in his work? He will stand before kings; he will not stand before obscure men. (Proverbs 22:29 ESV)

9. All Scripture is breathed out by God and profitable for teaching, for reproof, for correction, and for training in righteousness, (2 Timothy 3:16 ESV)

10. We know that our old self was crucified with him in order that the body of sin might be brought to nothing, so that we would no longer be enslaved to sin. (Romans 6:6 ESV)

11. But he answered, It is written, Man shall not live by bread alone, but by every word that comes from the mouth of God. (Matthew 4:4 ESV)

Scriptures on Fidelity:

1. For God so loved the world, that he gave his only begotten Son, that whosoever believeth in him should not perish, but have everlasting life. (John 3:16)

2. And be not conformed to this world: but be ye transformed by the renewing of your mind, that ye may prove what is that good, and acceptable, and perfect, will of God. (Romans 12:2)

3. I can do all things through Christ which strengtheneth me. (Philippians 4:13)

4. Finally, brethren, whatsoever things are true, whatsoever things are honest, whatsoever things are just, whatsoever things are pure, whatsoever things are lovely, whatsoever things are of good report; if there be any virtue, and if there be any praise, think on these things. (Philippians 4:8)

5. And we know that all things work together for good to them that love God, to them who are the called according to his purpose. (Romans 8:28)

6. If we confess our sins, he is faithful and just to forgive us our sins, and to cleanse us from all unrighteousness. (1 John 1:9)

7. And if it seem evil unto you to serve the Lord, choose you this day whom ye will serve; whether the gods which your fathers served that were on the other side of the flood, or the gods of the Amorites, in whose land ye dwell: but as for me and my house, we will serve the Lord. (Joshua 24:15)

8. For even hereunto were ye called: because Christ also suffered for us, leaving us an example, that ye should follow his steps: (1 Peter 2:21)

9. Greater love hath no man than this, that a man lay down his life for his friends. (John 15:13)

10. For with God nothing shall be impossible. (Luke 1:37)

Scriptures on Love:

1. But I say to you, love your enemies and pray for those who persecute you, (Matthew 5:44, NASB)

2. And He said to him, You shall Love the Lord your God with all your heart, and with all your soul, and with all your mind. (Matthew 22:37, NASB)

3. If you love those who love you, what credit is that to you? For even sinners love those who love them. (Luke 6:32, NASB)

4. By this all men will know that you are My disciples, if you have love for one another. (John 13:35, NASB)

5. If you love Me, you will keep My commandments. (John 14:15, NASB)

6. He who has My commandments and keeps them is the one who loves Me; and he who loves Me will be loved by My Father, and I will love him and will disclose Myself to him. (John 14:21, NASB)

7. Just as the Father has loved Me, I have also loved you; abide in My love. (John 15:9, NASB)

8. But God demonstrates His own love toward us, in that while we were yet sinners, Christ died for us. (Romans 5:8, NASB)

9. Let love be without hypocrisy. Abhor what is evil; cling to what is good. (Romans 12:9, NASB)

10. Love does no wrong to a neighbor; therefore, love is the fulfillment of the law. (Romans 13:10, NASB)

11. If I speak with the tongues of men and of angels, but do not have love, I have become a noisy gong or a clanging cymbal. (1 Corinthians 13:1, NASB)

12. Love is patient, love is kind and is not jealous; love does not brag and is not arrogant, (1 Corinthians 13:4, NASB)

13. Love never fails; but if there are gifts of prophecy, they will be done away; if there are tongues, they will cease; if there is knowledge, it will be done away. (1 Corinthians 13:8, NASB)

14. But now faith, hope, love, abide these three; but the greatest of these is love. (1 Corinthians 13:13, NASB)

15. We love, because He first loved us. (1 John 4:19, NASB)

Scriptures on Care:

1. But if anyone does not provide for his relatives, and especially for members of his household, he has denied the faith and is worse than an unbeliever. (1 Timothy 5:8 ESV)

2. Whoever closes his ear to the cry of the poor will himself call out and not be answered. (Proverbs 21:13 ESV)

3. And let us not grow weary of doing good, for in due season we will reap, if we do not give up. So then, as we have opportunity, let us do good to everyone, and especially to those who are of the household of faith. (Galatians 6:9-10 ESV)

4. And the King will answer them, 'Truly, I say to you, as you did it to one of the least of these my brothers, you did it to me. (Matthew 25:40 ESV)

5. Therefore encourage one another and build one another up, just as you are doing. (1 Thessalonians 5:11 ESV)

Scriptures Wisdom:

1. If any of you lacks wisdom, let him ask God, who gives generously to all without reproach, and it will be given him. (James 1:5 ESV)

2. But the wisdom from above is first pure, then peaceable, gentle, open to reason, full of mercy and good fruits, impartial and sincere. (James 3:17 ESV)

3. Blessed is the one who finds wisdom, and the one who gets understanding, for the gain from her is better than gain from silver and her profit better than gold. She is more precious than jewels, and nothing you desire can compare with her. Long life is in her right hand; in her left hand are riches and honor. Her ways are ways of pleasantness, and all her paths are peace... (Proverbs 3:13-18 ESV)

4. The fear of the LORD is the beginning of knowledge; fools despise wisdom and instruction. (Proverbs 1:7 ESV)

5. Listen to advice and accept instruction, that you may gain wisdom in the future. (Proverbs 19:20 ESV)

6. Look carefully then how you walk, not as unwise but as wise, making the best use of the time, because the days are evil. Therefore, do not be foolish, but understand what the will of the Lord is. (Ephesians 5:15-17 ESV)

7. The way of a fool is right in his own eyes, but a wise man listens to advice. (Proverbs 12:15 ESV)

8. Doing wrong is like a joke to a fool, but wisdom is pleasure to a man of understanding. (Proverbs 10:23 ESV)

9. Let the word of Christ dwell in you richly, teaching and admonishing one another in all wisdom, singing psalms and hymns and spiritual songs, with thankfulness in your hearts to God. (Colossians 3:16 ESV)

10. An intelligent heart acquires knowledge, and the ear of the wise seeks knowledge. (Proverbs 18:15 ESV)

11. For the LORD gives wisdom; from his mouth come knowledge and understanding; (Proverbs 2:6 ESV)

12. The fear of the LORD is the beginning of wisdom; all those who practice it have a good understanding. His praise endures forever! (Psalm 111:10 ESV)

13. Whoever restrains his words has knowledge, and he who has a cool spirit is a man of understanding. Even a fool who keeps silent is considered wise; when he closes his lips, he is deemed intelligent. (Proverbs 17:27-28 ESV)

14. How much better to get wisdom than gold! To get understanding is to be chosen rather than silver. (Proverbs 16:16 ESV)

Life Lesson 1

Learn The 10 Commandments

Life Lesson 1

Learn The 10 Commandments

For kids who are Pre-K to 6th grade and teenagers, they should know the 10 Commandments in the Bible early. Proverbs 22:6 says, "Train up a child in the way he should go and when he is old, he will not depart from it." The 10 Commandments are found in Exodus 20:1-17 and Deuteronomy 5:1-21.

I believe these principles are the foundation that introduce kids and teenagers to rules, laws and consequences. These 10 principles will also continue to be a guide throughout adulthood. The 10 Commandments are principles that guide us in our relationship with God and in our relationship with mankind.

The 10 Commandments are:

1. "I am the Lord your God, who brought you out of the land of Egypt, out of the house of bondage. You shall have no other gods before Me".

2. "You shall not make for yourself a carved image, or any likeness of anything that is in heaven above, or that is in the earth beneath, or that is in the water under the earth; you shall not bow down to them nor serve them. For I, the Lord your God, am a jealous God, visiting the iniquity of the fathers on the children to the third and fourth generations of those who hate Me, but showing mercy to thousands, to those who love Me and keep My Commandments."

3. "You shall not take the name of the Lord your God in vain, for the Lord will not hold him guiltless who takes His name in vain."

4. "Remember the Sabbath day, to keep it holy. Six days you shall labor and do all your work, but the seventh day is the Sabbath of the Lord your God. In it you shall do no work: you, nor your son, nor your daughter, nor your male servant, nor your female servant, nor your cattle, nor your stranger who is within your gates. For in six days the Lord made the heavens and the earth, the sea, and all that is in them,

and rested the seventh day. Therefore, the Lord blessed the Sabbath day and hallowed it."

5. "Honor your father and your mother, that your days may be long upon the land which the Lord your God is giving you."

6. "You shall not murder."

7. "You shall not commit adultery."

8. "You shall not steal."

9. "You shall not bear false witness against your neighbor."

10. "You shall not covet your neighbor's house; you shall not covet your neighbor's wife, nor his male servant, nor his female servant, nor his ox, nor his donkey, nor anything that is your neighbor's."

It should be mandatory that kids, teenagers and young adults know the 10 Commandments because some of them are embedded into our legal system which is our Penal Code. The Commandments thou shalt not kill, thou shalt not steal and thou shalt not bear false witness are represented in the Penal Code.

There are penalties or consequences for murder, theft, perjury and fraud. Every state has a penal code. In Texas it is called the Texas Penal Code. The training ground starts at home. As parents and guardians, if we start with these principles, they will help our kids, teens and young adults when they are faced with making right and wrong choices.

Discussion Questions:

1. What federal and state laws come from the 10 commandments?

2. Why were these laws given to mankind by God?

3. What happens when laws are not followed? What happens when laws are followed?

4. Why should you honor your father and mother?

5. Why are the 10 commandments important?

Bible Scriptures:

1. Exodus 20:3-17 - Thou shalt have no other gods before me.

2. Leviticus 22:31 -Therefore shall ye keep my commandments and do them: I am the LORD.

3. Matthew 5:17-22 - Think not that I am come to destroy the law, or the prophets: I am not come to destroy, but to fulfil.

4. Exodus 34:28 - And he was there with the LORD forty days and forty nights; he did neither eat bread, nor drink water. And he wrote upon the tables the words of the covenant, the ten commandments.

5. Deuteronomy 4:13 - And he declared unto you his covenant, which he commanded you to perform, even ten commandments; and he wrote them upon two tables of stone.

6. 1 John 2:3-6 - And hereby we do know that we know him, if we keep his commandments.

7. Romans 6:15 What then? shall we sin, because we are not under the law, but under grace? God forbid.

Life Lesson 2

Stay In A Child's Place

Life Lesson 2

Stay In A Child's Place

Kids should never take on issues that are for adults. They should get an adult to fight their battles. They should be respectful to all adults and stay in a child's place. Parents should teach their kids about safe and unsafe adults. Safe adults will do what is in the best interest of the child and teach kids the right and moral things to do. They will teach kids to honor and obey rules and they will give kids the tools to be successful in life. They will not steer kids down the wrong roads or lead them places that are dangerous for their lives. Safe and responsible adults will not give kids toxic information that will get them into trouble. Therefore, it is in children's best interest to mind their own business, live at peace with all men and expect to reap what they sow whether good or bad.

In order for kids to stay in a child's place they must be taught to mind their own business. In 1st Thessalonians 4:11 Paul instructs those at Thessalonica to aspire to lead a quiet life, to mind their own business and to work with their own hands, as commanded. The behavior that Paul teaches at Thessalonica should be a model example of how we should conduct our daily lives. Kids will avoid unnecessary troubles when they are taught to mind their own business.

A child should never battle or compete with an adult. It is disrespectful and shows lack of home training. Kids are protected when they stay in a child's place. It is never a good idea for kids to challenge an adult's authority. Adults have more knowledge and experience than kids. Kids should follow the rules and do what is expected of them. If they are being mistreated, they should tell an adult they trust to correct the matter.

When kids go toe to toe with an adult to compete, embarrass, or show off in front of their friends, they can become the target of an angry or disgruntle adult. It is best for kids to allow responsible adults to intervene and solve their problems with adults who mistreat them. Adults are more equipped to deal with other adults to solve issues. They can also take proper measures to hold other adults accountable.

When kids don't stay in a child's place they can sometimes be labeled as being too grown, fast or disrespectful. No matter what kids hear, see or learn about a grown person it is not their business. Kids should tell an adult they trust if there is a legitimate concern about another adult. They should never attempt to handle the situation by themselves. This can cause major problems for the child and can also put the child in danger. That's why kids should stay in the safety zone of being a kid.

Kids should also stay out of grown folks' battles. When an adult has beef with another adult that is not a child's battle. Some adults will get kids involved in their battles to get information on another adult. This is wicked and out of order. Parents, guardians and mentors should teach kids to stay out of grown folks' business and their personal battles. They will only get hurt in these situations.

Kids must also be taught there are consequences when they don't stay in a child's place. When they choose to be disrespectful, compete with adults and get into other people's business they will reap what they sow. Galatians 6:7 says, "Be not deceived; God is not mocked: for whatsoever a man soweth, that shall he also reap." Children must be taught early on that there are consequences for being messy.

It is best when kids are taught to live at peace with all men. They must be taught to get along with their peers and those they encounter. Romans 12:18 states "If it is possible, as far as it depends on you, live at peace with everyone." The bible teaches us principles on how to live and how we should treat others. When kids learn how to interact with others, they develop wisdom.

Discussion Questions:

1. Why should kids stay in a child's place?

2. What will happen if kids step out of their lane?

3. Is there ever a time a child should step out of their place as a child?

4. What happens when kids obey and stay in their lane?

5. Give examples of those that encourage kids to step out of a child's place?

Bible Scriptures:

1. Fathers, do not provoke your children to anger, but bring them up in the discipline and instruction of the Lord. (Ephesians 6:4)

2. Train up a child in the way he should go; even when he is old, he will not depart from it. (Proverbs 22:6 ESV)

3. Behold, children are a heritage from the LORD, the fruit of the womb a reward. Like arrows in the hand of a warrior are the children of one's youth. Blessed is the man who fills his quiver with them! He shall not be put to shame when he speaks with his enemies in the gate. (Psalm 127:3-5 ESV)

4. Children, obey your parents in the Lord, for this is right. "Honor your father and mother" (this is the first commandment with a promise), "that it may go well with you and that you may live long in the land." Fathers, do not provoke your children to anger, but bring them up in the discipline and instruction of the Lord. (Ephesians 6:1-4 ESV)

5. Whoever spares the rod hates his son, but he who loves him is diligent to discipline him. (Proverbs 13:24 ESV)

6. Folly is bound up in the heart of a child, but the rod of discipline drives it far from him. (Proverbs 22:15 ESV)

7. Behold, children are a heritage from the LORD, the fruit of the womb a reward. (Psalm 127:3 ESV)

8. Children, obey your parents in everything, for this pleases the Lord. (Colossians 3:20 ESV)

9. And they were bringing children to him that he might touch them, and the disciples rebuked them. But when Jesus saw it, he was indignant and said to them, "Let the children come to me; do not hinder them, for to such belongs the kingdom of God. Truly, I say to you, whoever does not receive the kingdom of God like a child shall not enter it." And he took them in his arms and blessed them, laying his hands on them. (Mark 10:13-16 ESV)

10. The rod and reproof give wisdom, but a child left to himself brings shame to his mother. (Proverbs 29:15 ESV)

11. Do not withhold discipline from a child; if you strike him with a rod, he will not die. If you strike him with the rod, you will save his soul from Sheol. (Proverbs 23:13-14 ESV)

12. Even a child makes himself known by his acts, by whether his conduct is pure and upright. (Proverbs 20:11 ESV)

Life Lesson 3
Obey God, Parents & Authority

Life Lesson 3

Obey God, Parents & Authority

When kids are born into this world parents should teach them obedience. They should learn the value and rewards of obedience. When kids follow rules, laws, and principles they will be successful in life. They will learn that rules are in place to keep them safe from harm. Choosing to follow rules, laws and principles is wise. This principle was taught in 1 Samuel 15:22 which states "And Samuel said, Has the LORD as great delight in burnt offerings and sacrifices, as in obeying the voice of the LORD? Behold, to obey is better than sacrifice, and to listen than the fat of rams." It is better to obey than to disobey. When we disobey, we must repent. We also need to ask God and those we sinned against to forgive us. Parents should teach their kids that consequences will follow when they are disobedient. Teaching kids there are consequences for breaking rules, laws and principles prepares them for life. Therefore, kids should be taught to obey God, parents, guardians and those in authority.

Kids should be taught to honor, reverence and obey God. Parents are responsible for teaching their kids about God, his statues, principles and laws. They should teach their children to obey God and his principles because obeying God provides a fulfilling life. God wants the best for us. He has a plan and destiny for each one of us. It is up to us to learn and obey his principles to reach our destiny.

We must obey God and do His WILL. "For you have need of patient endurance [to bear up under difficult circumstances without compromising], so that when you have carried out the will of God, you may receive *and* enjoy to the full what is promised. (Hebrews 10:36, Amplified Bible) We cannot skip over doing God's WILL to receive His promises. We do God's WILL and then we receive His promises. His WILL, purpose and assignments comes before us daily when we are used to help others who God puts in our path. Some are not experiencing the promises of God because they keep skipping over doing God's WILL.

Children should also be taught to obey their parents in the Lord for this is right, according to Ephesians 6:1. They should also be taught to honor their mother and father. Deuteronomy 5:16 says "Honor your father and your mother, as the LORD your God has commanded you, so that you may live long and that it may go well with you in the land the LORD your God is giving you." Parents are kids first authority. They enforce the rules, laws and consequences on kids. Teaching and enforcing rules and consequences is all a part of home training. The initial training ground for kids start at home. Their initial training shapes their behavior and teaches them how to function in and outside of the home. Parents should always start with teaching children God's principles and laws. Teaching children the Ten Commands is a good place to start.

They should also obey those who are in authority positions such as police officers, judges, teachers, principals, etc. Children should obey those in authority as long as they are telling them what is right. All adults should be telling children what is right and nothing wrong. Adults should be reported to the proper authorities if they are saying or doing anything to harm children. A child should always tell an adult they trust if someone is saying or doing anything to harm them.

Professional and legal authority exist to set boundaries and rules to protect us and keep us out of trouble. Kids are supposed to have some level of trust for individuals in these positions. Unfortunately, there are some good and bad apples in every industry and every profession. Our job is to shine the light on the bad apples. Report those who are not doing their job, those who are abusing their power and those who are doing illegal activities. We are also supposed to report those who are breaking the law under the disguise of their job title and position. We need to hold them accountable to face consequences, so they don't hurt people they are supposed to be protecting. We also want to purge these individuals out of the profession completely, so they don't ruin the reputation of the entire profession or industry.

Discussion Questions:

1. Who should kids obey and why?

2. How can kids show their obedience?

3. When should kids obey?

4. When should kids not obey?

5. What are some positive outcomes for kids' obedience?

6. What are some negative outcomes for kids' disobedience?

Bible Scriptures:

1. Obey your leaders and submit to them, for they are keeping watch over your souls, as those who will have to give an account. Let them do this with joy and not with groaning, for that would be of no advantage to you. (Hebrews 13:17 ESV)

2. Let every person be subject to the governing authorities. For there is no authority except from God, and those that exist have been instituted by God. (Romans 13:1 ESV)

3. Let every person be subject to the governing authorities. For there is no authority except from God, and those that exist have been instituted by God. Therefore, whoever resists the authorities resists what God has appointed, and those who resist will incur judgment. For rulers are not a terror to good conduct, but to bad. Would you have no fear of the one who is in authority? Then do what is good, and you will receive his approval, for he is God's servant for your good. But if you do wrong, be afraid, for he does not bear the sword in vain. For he is the servant of God, an avenger who carries out God's wrath on the wrongdoer. Therefore, one must be in subjection, not only to avoid God's wrath but also for the sake of conscience. ... (Romans 13:1-14 ESV)

4. Let every person be subject to the governing authorities. For there is no authority except from God, and those that exist have been instituted by God. Therefore, whoever resists the authorities resists what God has appointed, and those who resist will incur judgment. For rulers are not a terror to good conduct, but to bad. Would you have no fear of the one who is in authority? Then do what is good, and you will receive his approval, for he is God's servant for your good. But if you do wrong, be afraid, for he does not bear the sword in vain. For he is the servant of God, an avenger who carries out God's wrath on the wrongdoer. Therefore, one must be in subjection, not only to avoid God's wrath but also for the sake of conscience. ... (Romans 13:1-7 ESV)

5. But Peter and the apostles answered, "We must obey God rather than men. (Acts 5:29 ESV)

6. Remind them to be submissive to rulers and authorities, to be obedient, to be ready for every good work, (Titus 3:1 ESV)

7. For the husband is the head of the wife even as Christ is the head of the church, his body, and is himself its Savior. (Ephesians 5:23 ESV)

8. The natural person does not accept the things of the Spirit of God, for they are folly to him, and he is not able to understand them because they are spiritually discerned. (1 Corinthians 2:14 ESV)

9. I can do nothing on my own. As I hear, I judge, and my judgment is just, because I seek not my own will but the will of him who sent me. (John 5:30 ESV)

10. So, Jesus said to them, "Truly, truly, I say to you, the Son can do nothing of his own accord, but only what he sees the Father doing. For whatever the Father does, that the Son does likewise. (John 5:19 ESV)

11. And Jesus came and said to them, "All authority in heaven and on earth has been given to me. (Matthew 28:18 ESV)

Life Lesson 4
Show Appropriate Behavior

Life Lesson 4

Show Appropriate Behavior

When children are away from home they should be on their best behavior. Parents should require their kids to follow the rules and listen. It is a credit to parents and guardians when kids show appropriate behavior outside the home. Kids should always represent their parents, guardians and home in a positive manner. Children should also display respectful home training when they are away from their home environment. They should honor their parents, guardians and community.

Parents and guardians are responsible for teaching their kids obedience. The home environment is the initial training ground for kids to learn. The first set of rules kids should learn are the 10 commandments. They are moral principles that set the foundation for laws. Kids need to know how to function and follow rules. Children should be allowed to learn without judgement in a controlled environment. Parents should also teach and enforce consequences for breaking rules. The home should be where kids receive unconditional love, support and affirmation. Parents and guardians should reinforce moral principles, rules, and laws to prepare kids for life in and outside of the home.

It is important for kids to be good citizens at public functions. They should not be doing anything that is inappropriate. Kids should follow rules that are set for them. Parents should emphasize rules at home so kids can obey rules away from home. Kids should already know there are consequences when acting wild and unruly in formal settings. Kids learn that rules are important and disruptive behavior is not acceptable when parents, guardians, and teachers enforce consequences.

Kids should also show appropriate behavior at informal settings. They should practice respectful behavior during events. Children need to show their home training skills. They should sit down, be quiet and pay attention to the presentation or performance. If kids need something they should raise their hands to get the attention of the adult in charge. They should ask permission to leave their area to go to the restroom or get a drink of water. This allows the adult in charge to know the location of the kids they are watching.

Discussion Questions:

1. When should kids show appropriate behavior? Give examples.

2. What is appropriate behavior?

3. Why is it important for kids to show appropriate behavior?

4. What does showing appropriate behavior accomplish? Give examples.

5. Who is responsible for teaching kids appropriate behavior?

Bible Scriptures:

1. Do not be deceived: "Bad company ruins good morals. (1 Corinthians 15:33 ESV)

2. Keep your conduct among the Gentiles honorable, so that when they speak against you as evildoers, they may see your good deeds and glorify God on the day of visitation. (1 Peter 2:12 ESV)

3. For God gave us a spirit not of fear but of power and love and self-control. (2 Timothy 1:7 ESV)

4. Moreover, he must be well thought of by outsiders, so that he may not fall into disgrace, into a snare of the devil. (1 Timothy 3:7 ESV)

5. Therefore an overseer must be above reproach, the husband of one wife, sober-minded, self-controlled, respectable, hospitable, able to teach, (1 Timothy 3:2 ESV)

6. Likewise also that women should adorn themselves in respectable apparel, with modesty and self-control, not with braided hair and gold or pearls or costly attire, (1 Timothy 2:9 ESV)

7. First of all, then, I urge that supplications, prayers, intercessions, and thanksgivings be made for all people, for kings and all who are in high positions, that we may lead a peaceful and quiet life, godly and dignified in every way. This is good, and it is pleasing in the sight of God our Savior, who desires all people to be saved and to come to the knowledge of the truth. For there is one God, and there is one mediator between God and men, the man Christ Jesus, ... (1 Timothy 2:1-15 ESV)

8. If then you have been raised with Christ, seek the things that are above, where Christ is, seated at the right hand of God. Set your minds on things that are above, not on things that are on earth. For you have died, and your life is hidden with Christ in God. When Christ who is your life appears, then you also will appear with him in glory. Put to death therefore what is earthly in you: sexual immorality, impurity, passion, evil desire, and covetousness, which is idolatry. ... (Colossians 3:1-25 ESV)

9. Therefore, be imitators of God, as beloved children. And walk in love, as Christ loved us and gave himself up for us, a fragrant offering and sacrifice to God. But sexual immorality and all impurity or covetousness must not even be named among you, as is proper among saints. Let

there be no filthiness nor foolish talk nor crude joking, which are out of place, but instead let there be thanksgiving. For you may be sure of this, that everyone who is sexually immoral or impure, or who is covetous (that is, an idolater), has no inheritance in the kingdom of Christ and God. ... (Ephesians 5:1-33 ESV)

10. Or do you not know that your body is a temple of the Holy Spirit within you, whom you have from God? You are not your own, for you were bought with a price. So glorify God in your body. (1 Corinthians 6:19-20 ESV)

11. But I say to you that everyone who looks at a woman with lustful intent has already committed adultery with her in his heart. (Matthew 5:28 ESV)

Life Lesson 5

Don't Mistreat Others

Life Lesson 5

Don't Mistreat Others

Children should follow the Golden Rule "Treat Others As You Want To Be Treated." Kids need to learn this early in life because they will get the treatment they put out. They will make friends or enemies due to how they treat others. Kids need to learn this because it will help them develop positive relationships. This should also be taught to kids because the principle of reaping and sowing also applies. Kids need to know when they sow bad seeds of mistreatment of others, they will also reap mistreatment one day.

In Mark 12:30-31, Jesus was asked which commandment is the most important? He replied "The most important commandment is this: Listen, O Israel! The LORD our God is the one and only LORD. And you must love the LORD your God with all your heart, all your soul, all your mind, and all your strength. The second is equally important: Love your neighbor as yourself. No other commandment is greater than these." (NLT) We would not mistreat ourselves or like it if someone mistreated us. Parents should teach their kids not to bully or tease other kids. According to Janine Halloran in her book Social Skills for Kids, she says "It's a good reminder that approaching people in a kind, compassionate manner can have a positive outcome on social interactions. When you have a choice, choose kind." Parents should also teach their kids to speak up and say something when they see someone being bullied or teased. They should report and tell a responsible adult about the incident.

Parents should talk to their kids about the relationships they develop away from home and at school. They should teach their kids how to choose good friends and how to be a good friend. "To be a good and kind friend, you need to think about the other person's needs and wants. You can't always have it your way or be the one in charge all the time." (Halloran, 2018) Parents should teach their kids to make a difference in the world and make an impact on others. They should also teach their kids to do the right thing towards others. This also teaches kids accountability and how to hold others accountable.

Parent, guardians and mentors should also be an example of how to interact with others. They should model good behavior so kids can see what it looks like to treat others well. They need to know what it looks like to be kind and considerate of others. They should also hear what it sounds like to be polite and courteous to friends and strangers. It is important for parents, guardians and mentors to display the behavior they want imitated in various forms such as auditory, visual and kinesthetic.

Discussion Questions:

1. What do mistreating others mean?

2. Why should kids not mistreat others?

3. What is the opposite of mistreating others?

4. What can kids do to be helpful?

5. What are some reasons that kids mistreat others?

6. What should be done when kids are mistreating other kids?

Bible Scriptures:

1. After this I saw four angels standing at the four corners of the earth, holding back the four winds of the earth, that no wind might blow on earth or sea or against any tree. Then I saw another angel ascending from the rising of the sun, with the seal of the living God, and he called with a loud voice to the four angels who had been given power to harm earth and sea, saying, "Do not harm the earth or the sea or the trees, until we have sealed the servants of

our God on their foreheads." And I heard the number of the sealed, 144,000, sealed from every tribe of the sons of Israel: 12,000 from the tribe of Judah were sealed, 12,000 from the tribe of Reuben, 12,000 from the tribe of Gad, ... (Revelation 7:1-17 ESV)

2. And whenever you stand praying, forgive, if you have anything against anyone, so that your Father also who is in heaven may forgive you your trespasses. (Mark 11:25 ESV)

3. A dishonest man spreads strife, and a whisperer separates close friends. (Proverbs 16:28 ESV)

4. Then I looked, and behold, on Mount Zion stood the Lamb, and with him 144,000 who had his name and his Father's name written on their foreheads. And I heard a voice from heaven like the roar of many waters and like the sound of loud thunder. The voice I heard was like the sound of harpists playing on their harps, and they were singing a new song before the throne and before the four living creatures and before the elders. No one could learn that song except the 144,000 who had been redeemed from the earth. It is these who have not defiled themselves with women, for they are virgins. It is these who follow the Lamb wherever he goes. These have been redeemed from mankind as first fruits for God and the Lamb, and in their mouth no lie was found, for they are blameless. (Revelation 14:1-5 ESV)

5. They were told not to harm the grass of the earth or any green plant or any tree, but only those people who do not have the seal of God on their foreheads. (Revelation 9:4 ESV)

6. No temptation has overtaken you that is not common to man. God is faithful, and he will not let you be tempted beyond your ability, but with the temptation he will also provide the way of escape, that you may be able to endure it. (1 Corinthians 10:13 ESV)

7. Nor thieves, nor the greedy, nor drunkards, nor revilers, nor swindlers will inherit the kingdom of God. (1 Corinthians 6:10 ESV)

8. Or do you not know that the unrighteous will not inherit the kingdom of God? Do not be deceived: neither the sexually immoral, nor idolaters, nor adulterers, nor men who practice homosexuality, (1 Corinthians 6:9 ESV)

9. Bless those who persecute you; bless and do not curse them. (Romans 12:14 ESV)

10. A new commandment I give to you, that you love one another: just as I have loved you, you also are to love one another. By this all people will know that you are my disciples, if you have love for one another. (John 13:34-35 ESV)

11. But Jesus went to the Mount of Olives. Early in the morning he came again to the temple. All the people came to him, and he sat down and taught them. The scribes and the Pharisees brought a woman who had been caught in adultery and placing her in the midst they said to him, "Teacher, this woman has been caught in the act of adultery. Now in the Law Moses commanded us to stone such women. So, what do you say?" ... (John 8:1-11 ESV)

12. Then Peter came up and said to him, "Lord, how often will my brother sin against me, and I forgive him? As many as seven times?" Jesus said to him, "I do not say to you seven times, but seventy times seven. (Matthew 18:21-22 ESV)

13. For everything there is a season, and a time for every matter under heaven: (Ecclesiastes 3:1 ESV)

14. Whoever goes about slandering reveals secrets; therefore, do not associate with a simple babbler. (Proverbs 20:19 ESV)

15. You shall not bear false witness against your neighbor. (Exodus 20:16 ESV)

16. You shall not commit adultery. (Exodus 20:14 ESV)

17. You shall not murder. (Exodus 20:13 ESV)

18. As for you, you meant evil against me, but God meant it for good, to bring it about that many people should be kept alive, as they are today. (Genesis 50:20 ESV)

Life Lesson 6
Respect Others & Property

Life Lesson 6

Respect Others & Property

It is very important that kids learn to respect other people, their property and things. This will cut down on a lot of chaos. It will also help kids to get along with others. Respecting others and their things helps to maintain order. When kids respect others and their property it also enforces the commandment and principle "Thou Shalt Not Steal." Kids should not touch, take property or things that belong to others without their permission. This teaches kids boundaries and how to respect other people's boundaries. When kids learn the principle of respecting other people's property, they will avoid being accused of taking and stealing. They need to know because stealing is a crime, and they can be prosecuted for the crime of stealing.

I was taught at an early age by my aunt Rosie Marie Willis that no one in this world owes me anything. If someone helped me, it was because they wanted to not because they had to. This advice can also go both ways. No one owes you anything and you do not owe others anything. Respecting ourselves and others covers lots of different behaviors. One thing that respect means is using manners, like saying please and thank you, and being polite to the people around you. It means being honest while being kind. (Halloran, 2018)

Janine Halloran further states, "It's also important to recognize that while people may look different, or come from different places, we are all still human, and should be treated equally with respect. You can always find common ground with someone even when they are different from you. Kids should be taught not to steal or take anything from others. Just because you want something that someone else has does not give you the right to take it. It is nothing wrong with wanting nice things. The responsible thing to do is work hard and acquire things for yourself. Get what others have the legal and responsible way by working hard for it. Kids should also ask their parents to buy what they want if they are underage without a job.

Discussion Questions:

1. What is respect?

2. How can you show that you are respecting others and their property?

3. What are some examples of kids not respecting others and their property?

4. Why is it important to respect others and their property?

5. What are some examples of personal property?

Bible Scriptures:

1. Likewise, husbands, live with your wives in an understanding way, showing honor to the woman as the weaker vessel, since they are heirs with you of the grace of life, so that your prayers may not be hindered. (1 Peter 3:7 ESV)

2. Honor everyone. Love the brotherhood. Fear God. Honor the emperor. (1 Peter 2:17 ESV)

3. Honor your father and your mother, that your days may be long in the land that the LORD your God is giving you. (Exodus 20:12 ESV)

4. For the wages of sin is death, but the free gift of God is eternal life in Christ Jesus our Lord. (Romans 6:23 ESV)

5. The thief comes only to steal and kill and destroy. I came that they may have life and have it abundantly. (John 10:10 ESV)

6. Blessed shall he be who takes your little ones and dashes them against the rock! (Psalm 137:9 ESV)

Life Lesson 7
Listen & Follow Directions

Life Lesson 7

Listen & Follow Directions

Kids need to simply learn how to follow directions without talking back. They should not be talking, giving their feedback or interrupting when directions are being given. The directions given could be the information that saves a child's life. Adults give directions to move things forward while staying on track with mandatory tasks.

It's important for kids to be quiet and listen. Adults don't want kids to miss important information that can help them. It is also equally important for kids to obey the directions. They should listen and follow the instructions of the adult in charge to keep them safe. Listening according to dictionary.com is to pay attention, heed and obey. Parents should teach their kids at home to listen, follow directions, rules and procedures.

Following rules and directions is expected of children in and outside the home. Children are expected to follow rules and directions at school, church, and other formal events. Children should remember their home training and obey rules and directions. A critical skill for positive social interactions is following directions. It is important for kids to listen, internalize information, process it and align their behavior with the information. (Halloran, 2018)

Parents should also teach their kids about safe and unsafe adults. They should make it clear when children should follow rules and directions and when they should not. Following common directions such as street signs and environmental print should be required. Children should also follow directions when there is an emergency. They also need to know what to embrace and what to avoid. It is equally important when kids should not follow directions. For example, kids should not follow the directions of a stranger. They should not blindly follow directions of anyone who is trying to lead them away to harm them. They should never go with a stranger or anyone they do not trust no matter what excuse is given. (Halloran, 2018)

Discussion Questions:

1. Why is it important to listen and follow directions?

2. What are some examples of an adult giving directions?

3. What actions show that kids are listening and following directions?

4. What are directions?

5. How do adults know that kids are listening and following directions?

Bible Scriptures:

1. Jesus said to him, "I am the way, and the truth, and the life. No one comes to the Father except through me. (John 14:6 ESV)

2. A Psalm of David. The LORD is my shepherd; I shall not want. He makes me lie down in green pastures. He leads me beside still waters. He restores my soul. He leads me in paths of righteousness for his name's sake. Even though I walk through the valley of the shadow of death, I will fear no evil, for you are with me; your rod and your staff, they comfort me. You prepare a table before me in the presence of my enemies; you anoint my head with oil; my cup overflows. ... (Psalm 23:1-6 ESV)

3. For whoever keeps the whole law but fails in one point has become accountable for all of it. (James 2:10 ESV)

4. "All things are lawful for me," but not all things are helpful. "All things are lawful for me," but I will not be enslaved by anything. (1 Corinthians 6:12 ESV)

5. When the day of Pentecost arrived, they were all together in one place. And suddenly there came from heaven a sound like a mighty rushing wind, and it filled the entire house where they were sitting. And divided tongues as of fire appeared to them and rested on each one of them. And they were all filled with the Holy Spirit and began to speak in other tongues as the Spirit gave them utterance. Now there were dwelling in Jerusalem Jews, devout men from every nation under heaven. ... (Acts 2:1-47 ESV)

6. In the first book, O Theophilus, I have dealt with all that Jesus began to do and teach, (Acts 1:1 ESV)

7. When they had finished breakfast, Jesus said to Simon Peter, "Simon, son of John, do you love me more than these?" He said to him, "Yes, Lord; you know that I love you." He said to him, "Feed my lambs." He said to him a second time, "Simon, son of John, do you love me?" He said to him, "Yes, Lord; you know that I love you." He said to him, "Tend my sheep." He said to him the third time, "Simon, son of John, do you love me?" Peter was grieved because he said to him the third time, "Do you love me?" and he said to him, "Lord, you know everything; you know that I love you." Jesus said to him, "Feed my sheep. Truly,

truly, I say to you, when you were young, you used to dress yourself and walk wherever you wanted, but when you are old, you will stretch out your hands, and another will dress you and carry you where you do not want to go." (This he said to show by what kind of death he was to glorify God.) And after saying this he said to him, "Follow me." ... (John 21:15-20 ESV)

8. But the Helper, the Holy Spirit, whom the Father will send in my name, he will teach you all things and bring to your remembrance all that I have said to you. (John 14:26 ESV)

9. So, Jesus said to them, "Truly, truly, I say to you, unless you eat the flesh of the Son of Man and drink his blood, you have no life in you. (John 6:53 ESV)

10. And behold, a lawyer stood up to put him to the test, saying, "Teacher, what shall I do to inherit eternal life?" He said to him, "What is written in the Law? How do you read it?" And he answered, "You shall love the Lord your God with all your heart and with all your soul and with all your strength and with all your mind, and your neighbor as yourself." And he said to him, "You have answered correctly; do this, and you will live." But he, desiring to justify himself, said to Jesus, "And who is my neighbor?" ... (Luke 10:25-37 ESV)

11. And as he was setting out on his journey, a man ran up and knelt before him and asked him, "Good Teacher, what must I do to inherit eternal life?" And Jesus said to him, "Why do you call me good? No one is good except God alone. You know the commandments: 'Do not murder, Do not commit adultery, Do not steal, Do not bear false witness, Do not defraud, Honor your father and mother.'" And he said to him, "Teacher, all these I have kept from my youth." And Jesus, looking at him, loved him, and said to him, "You lack one thing: go, sell all that you have and give to the poor, and you will have treasure in heaven; and come, follow me." ... (Mark 10:17-31 ESV)

12. That same day Jesus went out of the house and sat beside the sea. And great crowds gathered about him, so that he got into a boat and sat down. And the whole crowd stood on the beach. And he told them many things in parables, saying: "A sower went out to sow. And as he sowed, some seeds fell along the path, and the birds came and devoured them. Other seeds fell on rocky ground, where they did not have much soil, and immediately they sprang up, since they had no depth of soil, ... (Matthew 13:1-58 ESV)

13. Teach me your way, O LORD, that I may walk in your truth; unite my heart to fear your name. (Psalm 86:11 ESV)

Life Lesson 8
Tell If Someone Hurts You

Life Lesson 8

Tell If Someone Hurts You

Parents should always teach their kids to tell them or a responsible adult if someone hurts them. It is unfortunate that there are adults who are unsafe in all walks of life. They exist in every family, community, profession, industry, institution, and generation. Adults are supposed to model, teach and protect children who are in their care. They are supposed to help kids and resolve problems. They are not supposed to create problems. Adults should be responsible, mature and do what is right.

All adults are subject to the laws of the land and are subject to God. The laws of the land and the principles of God should be enough to convict every adult to do the right thing by children. Unfortunately, following the laws of the land and God's principles are not automatic. Following what is right begins with the heart of man. When adults have other motives and hidden agendas in the heart children get hurt or injured. Unregenerated men and women who do not honor God, the Bible or the laws of the land are unsafe to families, communities, industries, professions, institutions, generations and future generations. When there is an unsafe adult anywhere, they are a part of the problem and not the solution.

Kids should feel safe when they are in the care of responsible adults. Kids should not feel afraid when they are cared for by adults. Parents should teach their kids to tell an adult that will help them to stop the person that is causing harm to them. Many kids have been hurt, abused emotionally and physically and even sexually molested by someone they trusted. When the trust has been violated, kids should tell their parents or another responsible adult.

In Luke 17:1-2, Jesus told his disciples "It is inevitable that stumbling blocks will come, but woe to the one through whom they come! It would be better for him to have a millstone hung around his neck and to be thrown into the sea than to cause one of these little ones to stumble." God takes it seriously when someone plots the demise of others by setting up stumbling blocks for them to fall.

According to Erik Erikson, psychological development from infancy to old age includes eight stages. In the infant stage which is 0 to 1 years old a child is forming basic trust and mistrust which influences social and emotional development. Hope and optimism are developed during this stage. The mother's relationship with the child is a priority. The mother provides love and constant care to help the child develop trust. (McLeod, 2018)

When unsafe adults hurt children there should be outrage. There should also be consequences for the perpetrator and healing for the victim. The outrage should be worked out by using the laws of the land to bring justice. Things should be done decent and in order. One of the most important key things to remember and hold on to is Romans 12:19 which states "Never take your own revenge, beloved, but leave room for the wrath *of God,* for it is written: "VENGEANCE IS MINE, I WILL REPAY," says the Lord. We have to trust God that He will make things right and He will set the record straight. He will punish those who have caused hurt to others.

Even though God does not want us to take our own revenge into our own hands by carrying out the punishment we feel they should get, it is nothing wrong with utilizing the justice system and institutions to bring about justice.

Discussion Questions:

1. Who should kids tell when they get hurt?

2. Why should kids tell if someone hurts them?

3. What are some ways kids can get hurt?

4. When should kids tell when someone hurts them?

5. Why is it important to tell if someone hurts kids?

Bible Scriptures:

1. After this I saw four angels standing at the four corners of the earth, holding back the four winds of the earth, that no wind might blow on earth or sea or against any tree. Then I saw another angel ascending from the rising of the sun, with the seal of the living God, and he called with a loud voice to the four angels who had been given power to harm earth and sea, saying, "Do not harm the earth or the sea or the trees, until we have sealed the servants of our God on their foreheads." And I heard the number of the sealed, 144,000, sealed from every tribe of the sons of Israel: 12,000 from the tribe of Judah were sealed, 12,000 from the tribe of Reuben, 12,000 from the tribe of Gad, ... (Revelation 7:1-17 ESV)

2. And whenever you stand praying, forgive, if you have anything against anyone, so that your Father also who is in heaven may forgive you your trespasses. (Mark 11:25 ESV)

3. A dishonest man spreads strife, and a whisperer separates close friends. (Proverbs 16:28 ESV)

4. Then I looked, and behold, on Mount Zion stood the Lamb, and with him 144,000 who had his name and his Father's name written on their foreheads. And I heard a voice from heaven like the roar of many waters and like the sound of loud thunder. The voice I heard was like the sound of harpists playing on their harps, and they were

singing a new song before the throne and before the four living creatures and before the elders. No one could learn that song except the 144,000 who had been redeemed from the earth. It is these who have not defiled themselves with women, for they are virgins. It is these who follow the Lamb wherever he goes. These have been redeemed from mankind as first fruits for God and the Lamb, and in their mouth no lie was found, for they are blameless. (Revelation 14:1-5 ESV)

5. They were told not to harm the grass of the earth or any green plant or any tree, but only those people who do not have the seal of God on their foreheads. (Revelation 9:4 ESV)

6. No temptation has overtaken you that is not common to man. God is faithful, and he will not let you be tempted beyond your ability, but with the temptation he will also provide the way of escape, that you may be able to endure it. (1 Corinthians 10:13 ESV)

7. Nor thieves, nor the greedy, nor drunkards, nor revilers, nor swindlers will inherit the kingdom of God. (1 Corinthians 6:10 ESV)

8. Or do you not know that the unrighteous will not inherit the kingdom of God? Do not be deceived: neither the sexually immoral, nor idolaters, nor adulterers, nor men who practice homosexuality, (1 Corinthians 6:9 ESV)

9. Bless those who persecute you; bless and do not curse them. (Romans 12:14 ESV)

10. A new commandment I give to you, that you love one another: just as I have loved you, you also are to love one another. By this all people will know that you are my disciples, if you have love for one another. (John 13:34-35 ESV)

11. But Jesus went to the Mount of Olives. Early in the morning he came again to the temple. All the people came to him, and he sat down and taught them. The scribes and the Pharisees brought a woman who had been caught in adultery and placing her in the midst they said to him, "Teacher, this woman has been caught in the act of adultery. Now in the Law Moses commanded us to stone such women. So, what do you say?" ... (John 8:1-11 ESV)

12. Then Peter came up and said to him, "Lord, how often will my brother sin against me, and I forgive him? As many as seven times?" Jesus said to him, "I do not say to you seven times, but seventy times seven. (Matthew 18:21-22 ESV)

13. But I say to you, Do not resist the one who is evil. But if anyone slaps you on the right cheek, turn to him the other also. (Matthew 5:39 ESV)

14. For everything there is a season, and a time for every matter under heaven: (Ecclesiastes 3:1 ESV)

15. Whoever goes about slandering reveals secrets; therefore, do not associate with a simple babbler. (Proverbs 20:19 ESV)

16. You shall not bear false witness against your neighbor. (Exodus 20:16 ESV)

17. You shall not commit adultery. (Exodus 20:14 ESV)

18. You shall not murder. (Exodus 20:13 ESV)

19. As for you, you meant evil against me, but God meant it for good, to bring it about that many people should be kept alive, as they are today. (Genesis 50:20 ESV)

Life Lesson 9

Seek Worthy Mentors

Life Lesson 9

Seek Worthy Mentors

Kids should seek mentors they trust. Worthy mentors require good moral character and integrity. According to dictionary.com, a mentor is a wise and trusted counselor or teacher. In Titus 2:1-6, the older men are admonished to train up the younger men and the older women should train up the younger women. It is important that older men and women protect and take our youth under our wings. Where no counsel is, the people fall: but in the multitude of counsellers there is safety. (Proverbs 11:14, KJV)

Kids need someone who has their best interest. This is also true about babes in Christ. When new converts repent and turn away from a life of sin, accept Jesus Christ as their Lord and Savior and decide to live according to God's word, they will need mentoring, prayer and support on their new journey.

It is important for new Christians to become a part of a local church where they can serve, learn about God's word and grow to spiritual maturity. New Christians should have a network of Seasoned Believers who support, mentor and pray for them. Studying the word of God is an ongoing responsibility for all Christians. According to 2 Timothy 2:15 the Bible says "Study to shew thyself approved unto God, a workman that needeth not to be ashamed, rightly dividing the word of truth. In order for us to develop into spiritual maturity we must continue to read and study God's word. We must know the Bible so we can apply it to our lives.

Kids and babes in Christ need mentors who do not practice hypocrisy. Worthy mentors should have absolute biblical standards they live by. They value truth and fear God. They teach those they mentor standards and principles that are based on truth and measured against the Bible. Worthy mentors do not teach one thing and do the opposite. They do not say one thing out of their mouths and their actions or behavior does opposite. Their talk must line up with their walk. A mentor's life should match their principles and standards. If a mentor's life, behavior, and actions don't match what they speak out their mouth be cautious. Do not choose that mentor.

It is imperative that kids, teens, and young adults learn to choose worthy mentors. When kids choose to follow and pattern their lives after someone it can be a blessing or a curse. It can be a blessing when they model and give advice that will bring blessings, rewards and progress. It will be a stronghold or curse if the mentor's advice, behavior, patterns and habits are toxic. The bad influence brings strongholds, curses, consequences, regrets and set-backs. It is wise to be cautious when choosing a mentor.

Discussion Questions:

1. What is a mentor?

2. What are the characteristics of a worthy mentor?

3. Why should kids be careful when choosing a mentor?

4. What is the responsibility of a mentor?

5. Why do kids need mentors?

Bible Scriptures:

1. Train up a child in the way he should go; even when he is old he will not depart from it. (Proverbs 22:6 ESV)

2. Without counsel plans fail, but with many advisers they succeed. (Proverbs 15:22 ESV)

3. Your testimonies are my delight; they are my counselors. (Psalm 119:24 ESV)

4. All Scripture is breathed out by God and profitable for teaching, for reproof, for correction, and for training in righteousness, (2 Timothy 3:16 ESV)

5. The purpose in a man's heart is like deep water, but a man of understanding will draw it out. (Proverbs 20:5 ESV)

6. For no good tree bears bad fruit, nor again does a bad tree bear good fruit, for each tree is known by its own fruit. For figs are not gathered from thornbushes, nor are grapes picked from a bramble bush. The good person out of the good treasure of his heart produces good, and the evil person out of his evil treasure produces evil, for out of the abundance of the heart his mouth speaks. (Luke 6:43-45 ESV)

7. For God is not a God of confusion but of peace. As in all the churches of the saints, 1 (Corinthians 14:33 ESV)

8. For the word of God is living and active, sharper than any two-edged sword, piercing to the division of soul and of spirit, of joints and of marrow, and discerning the thoughts and intentions of the heart. (Hebrews 4:12 ESV)

9. I have stored up your word in my heart, that I might not sin against you. (Psalm 119:11 ESV)

Life Lesson 10
Don't Model Bad Habits

Life Lesson 10

Don't Model Bad Habits

Parents, guardians and mentors should teach good habits to kids. They need to know the difference between copying a good habit verses a bad habit. Kids are very impressionable because of their age and lack of life experiences. They don't have the maturity, knowledge or wisdom that comes over time. They are just getting started.

Parents, guardians and mentors should stress to kids not to follow bad habits of others. It doesn't matter if a person has an important title, money, big house, nice car, or desired material things. The bad habits and behaviors of others should not be followed. Kids are not required to follow bad habits and behaviors to obtain the things they desire. God's way is the only way to obtain true blessings and true riches. Matthew 6:33 says "But seek ye first the kingdom of God, and his righteousness; and all these things shall be added unto you." (KJV)

Do not be misled: "Bad company corrupts good character." (1 Corinthians 15:33, NIV) Bad company is anyone who teaches you to do wrong, disobey your parents or disobey God. These people do not have a kid's best interest at heart. They don't care if a kid is destroyed, and their life is left in shambles. Bad company are those who only care about themselves. They don't think about the poisoned advice they give to others. Parents should teach their kids not to put their trust in people but only in God. God will not disappoint or hurt kids. God is not human, that he should lie, not a human being, that he should change his mind. Does he speak and then not act? Does he promise and not fulfill? (Numbers 23:19)

Discernment should be used when taking advice from anyone. Make sure a person's advice has been successful in their life before following their example. Don't take advice from someone who is failing in the area where they are giving advice. They should experience success with the advice they give. If they are unsuccessful in the area, they are giving advice that is a red flag.

Using discernment involves looking at someone's actions, behavior and lifestyle. If their habits, behavior, actions or lifestyle leads to criminal activity don't model that behavior. If the habits can get you in trouble and leads you down the wrong road do not model that behavior. Any behavior or habits that are dark, deceitful, evil and wicked, criminal and unfruitful don't model it. Ephesians 5:11

states, "Take no part in the unfruitful works of darkness, but instead expose them."

Parents, guardians and mentors are doing a disservice to kids by keeping them in the dark about potential dangers and about life. Educate kids and go over with them different scenarios about real life. Go over issues that commonly happen in families and communities. Don't leave kids prey to Satan. Eliminate Satan's opportunity to educate your kids first. Do not allow the devil to present a toxic, pseudo, false, dangerous and deceptive truth to them. Every parent should arm their kids with the truth which should be rooted in the word of God found in the Bible. When kids know the absolute truth, they can discard all advice that is opposite of the truth. All advice should be measured against the word of God. God's word is TRUTH. Sanctify them by the truth; your word is truth. (John 17:17)

Parents teach your kids to follow the example of the man in Psalm 1. Blessed is the man that walketh not in the counsel of the ungodly, nor standeth in the way of sinners, nor sitteth in the seat of the scornful. But his delight is in the law of the LORD; and in his law doth he meditate day and night. And he shall be like a tree planted by the rivers of water, that bringeth forth his fruit in his season; his leaf also shall not wither; and whatsoever he doeth shall prosper. The ungodly are not so: but are like the chaff which the wind driveth away. Therefore, the ungodly shall not stand in the judgment, nor sinners in the congregation of the righteous. For the LORD knoweth the way of the righteous: but the way of the ungodly shall perish. When kids follow toxic and ungodly advice, they will reap the consequences of that ungodly advice. However, when kids learn to recognize and follow godly examples, they will be blessed.

Discussion Questions:

1. What are bad habits? Give examples.

2. Why should kids not follow bad habits?

3. How do bad habits affect kids?

4. Give examples of those who practice and model bad habits to kids?

5. What is the opposite of bad habits? Give examples.

Bible Scriptures:

1. Do not be conformed to this world, but be transformed by the renewal of your mind, that by testing you may discern what is the will of God, what is good and acceptable and perfect. (Romans 12:2 ESV)

2. No temptation has overtaken you that is not common to man. God is faithful, and he will not let you be tempted beyond your ability, but with the temptation he will also provide the way of escape, that you may be able to endure it. (1 Corinthians 10:13 ESV)

3. If we confess our sins, he is faithful and just to forgive us our sins and to cleanse us from all unrighteousness. (1 John 1:9 ESV)

4. Do not be anxious about anything, but in everything by prayer and supplication with thanksgiving let your requests be made known to God. And the peace of God, which surpasses all understanding, will guard your hearts and your minds in Christ Jesus. Finally, brothers, whatever is true, whatever is honorable, whatever is just, whatever is pure, whatever is lovely, whatever is commendable, if there is any excellence, if there is anything worthy of praise, think about these things. (Philippians 4:6-8 ESV)

5. Submit yourselves therefore to God. Resist the devil, and he will flee from you. (James 4:7 ESV)

6. Let no one despise you for your youth, but set the believers an example in speech, in conduct, in love, in faith, in purity. (1 Timothy 4:12 ESV)

7. Because, if you confess with your mouth that Jesus is Lord and believe in your heart that God raised him from the dead, you will be saved. (Romans 10:9 ESV)

8. Keep your life free from love of money, and be content with what you have, for he has said, "I will never leave you nor forsake you." (Hebrews 13:5 ESV)

9. And he said, "What comes out of a person is what defiles him. For from within, out of the heart of man, come evil thoughts, sexual immorality, theft, murder, adultery, coveting, wickedness, deceit, sensuality, envy, slander, pride, foolishness. All these evil things come from within, and they defile a person." (Mark 7:20-23 ESV)

10. Casting all your anxieties on him, because he cares for you. (1 Peter 5:7 ESV)

11. How can a young man keep his way pure? By guarding it according to your word. (Psalm 119:9 ESV)

12. For the love of money is a root of all kinds of evils. It is through this craving that some have wandered away from the faith and pierced themselves with many pangs. (1 Timothy 6:10 ESV)

13. For God gave us a spirit not of fear but of power and love and self-control. (2 Timothy 1:7 ESV)

14. Or do you not know that your body is a temple of the Holy Spirit within you, whom you have from God? You are not your own, (1 Corinthians 6:19 ESV)

15. Or do you not know that the unrighteous will not inherit the kingdom of God? Do not be deceived: neither the sexually immoral, nor idolaters, nor adulterers, nor men who practice homosexuality, nor thieves, nor the greedy, nor drunkards, nor revilers, nor swindlers will inherit the kingdom of God. And such were some of you. But you were washed, you were sanctified, you were justified in the name of the Lord Jesus Christ and by the Spirit of our God. (1 Corinthians 6:9-11 ESV)

16. Little children, let us not love in word or talk but in deed and in truth. (1 John 3:18 ESV)

17. "All things are lawful for me," but not all things are helpful. "All things are lawful for me," but I will not be enslaved by anything. (1 Corinthians 6:12 ESV)

18. I appeal to you therefore, brothers, by the mercies of God, to present your bodies as a living sacrifice, holy and acceptable to God, which is your spiritual worship. (Romans 12:1 ESV)

19. For God so loved the world, that he gave his only Son, that whoever believes in him should not perish but have eternal life. (John 3:16 ESV)

Conclusion

Conclusion

The absolute standard is God's word. God's principles in the Bible should be used to measure all content, facts and knowledge. No matter what arguments philosophers present, the word of God is true. When philosophers honor and submit to God in their research they will educate and impact the masses. John 17:17 testifies "Sanctify them through thy truth: thy word is truth." (KJV) God's principles coupled with the Holy Spirit will guide us into all truth. John 16:13 confirms "However, when He, the Spirit of truth, has come, He will guide you into all truth; for He will not speak on His own *authority,* but whatever He hears He will speak; and He will tell you things to come." (NKJV)

It is important to know what is happening at the different stages of development of a child to adulthood. Parents, guardians and mentors can help guide and have a positive impact on the child if they are knowledgeable in training and modeling the different stages of a child's life. Parents, guardians and mentors should pray and ask God to help guide them as they guide those who are under their direct leadership.

Parents, guardians, and mentors should pay attention to the development of your child during the kid stage. Protect and guide them in the right direction and steer them down the right path. Help them grow and develop so they can become all that God has planned for their purpose on earth. Help to block any toxic, unhealthy, dangerous, evil, and demonic forces that try to hinder, handicap, derail, abort or become a stronghold to prevent them from going forward with God's purpose for their lives. Encourage and do everything within your power to help each child mature and develop mentally, psychologically, physically and spiritually on the way to their destiny.

Bibliography

Bibliography

Halloran, J. (2018). *Social Skills for kids over 75 fun games and activities for building better relationships, problem solving and improving communication*. PESI.

McLeod, S. A. (2018, May 03). Erik Erikson's stages of psychosocial development. Simply psychology: https://www.simplypsychology.org/Erik-Erikson.html

Mishra, P., & Singh, S. (2019). Jean Piaget's Theory of Cognitive Development. Global Journal for Research Analysis, Vol. 8 (Issue 7), p. 1-2.

Tabula Rasa. (2020, January 15). *New World Encyclopedia,* Retrieved 19:05, September 8, 2022 from https://www.newworldencyclopedia.org/p/index.php?title=Tabula_rasa&oldid=1030794.

Dictionary.com

Biblehub.com

Openbible.info/topics

About The Author

About The Author

Brenda Diann Johnson was born in Dallas, Texas on September 14, 1970, to Robert Johnson and Thelma Byrd. She is the oldest of five children. She has a brother, sister, and two half-brothers.

Brenda received her education from the Dallas and Wharton, Texas school systems. She graduated from Government, Law, and Law Enforcement Magnet High School in Dallas. She also received her Bachelor of Arts degree in Communications (Broadcast News) from UTA in Arlington, Texas and her Master of Education Degree from Strayer University. She has her Texas license in Life, Health, Accident & HMO insurance, her Texas Adjusters License in All Lines and she is a Texas Notary Public.

Today, Brenda is the CEO/Founder of The Young Scholar's Book Club and ASWIFTT ENTERPRISES, LLC. She is an experienced educator who has taught and tutored Pre-K through College. Brenda is the Dean of Education, Curriculum & Instruction for Best Practices Training Institute. (B.P.T.I.) She has also authored books and articles.

From 2001 to 2002, Brenda served as the chairperson for an entrepreneur group called STEP (Sowing Toward Everlasting Prosperity) and a Center Leader for the Plan Fund. Brenda also served as Co-Founder of ASWIFTT Writer's Guild from 2010 to 2019.

In the community, Brenda has served as a volunteer to organizations that help AIDS, HIV, and Syphilis patients. She currently lives in Texas with her family.

Books and Services at brendadiannjohnson.com

ASWIFTT ENTERPRISES, LLC

Business advertising for Print & Media

BOOK PUBLISHING

RADIO

T.V.

Newspaper

We have affordable advertising packages in our media categories. Some Ads are as low as $35.00.

You can visit us online at: www.aswifttbooks.com or e-mail us at: aswifttbookpublishing@yahoo.com

ASWIFTT BOOKS

(Ambassadors Sent With Information For This Time)

ASWIFTT ENTERPRISES, LLC creates businesses that write and publish content in all three (3) media genres such as radio, tv and newspaper that focus on delivering timely, newsworthy and accurate news stories. The media genres also report on local, regional, national and international topics.

The Young Scholar's Workbook: Book I Vol. I
(www.tysbookclub.com)

The Young Scholar's Workbook: Book I Vol. I is a fundraiser publication for The Young Scholar's Book Club. 50% of the proceeds go to help keep mentoring and tutoring services free to students. $19.95 plus s/h

Advertise in

ASWIFTT BOOKS

Your business will have a permanent advertising spot in an ASWIFTT Book. The book that carries your Business Ad will continue to advertise your business every time the book is printed and purchased by a customer. For information on book advertising email us at: aswifttbookpublishing@yahoo.com

$35.00 Business Ad
Includes:
1. Business Name
2. Address

$100.00 Business Ad
Includes:
1. Logo
2. Business Name
3. Address
4. Phone Number
5. Website
6. Short Bio

$65.00 Business Ad
Includes:
1. Logo
2. Business Name
3. Address
4. Phone Number
5. Website

ASWIFTT ENTERPRISES, LLC ORDER FORM

Name _____

Address _____

City _____

State _____

Zip _____

Item _____ Amount _____

Item _____ Amount _____

Item _____ Amount _____

Add $8.50 for Shipping and Handling on books

Total: _____

Make Checks, Money Orders, Cashier's Checks out to:

ASWIFTT ENTERPRISES, LLC

P.O. Box 380669

Duncanville, Texas 75138

Credit Card Orders:

Circle One: Master Card   Visa   American Express   Discover

Credit Card Number _____

Exp. Date _____

Three Digit Security Number on back of Card _____

Name & Address Associated with Credit Card:

_____   Email: _____

_____   _____

Authorization Signature   Date

Your order will be processed or shipped 2 to 4 weeks from the date order is received. Direct concerns on orders email: aswifttbookpublishing@yahoo.com

Thank you for your business! Make copies of this form.

www.ingramcontent.com/pod-product-compliance
Lightning Source LLC
Chambersburg PA
CBHW081324040426
42453CB00013B/2296